# Coffee and Esp

## Make Your Favorite

> Author: Tanja Dusy | Photos: Jörn Rynio

# Contents

## Fundamentals

➤ 4   Everything You Need to Know
➤ 6   The Right Way to Make Coffee
   7   Four International Classics
   8   Making Espresso
   9   Flavoring Coffee

## Recipes

10   Just Coffee—But a Favorite Around the World: Served Hot or Cold, from Latte Macchiato to Mocha Flip

28   Made with Coffee—Desserts and a Variety of Snacks: Sweet Tidbits with a Fine Coffee Aroma

42   Served with Coffee—International Snacks, or Everything that Tastes Good with Coffee from Around the World

## Appendix

➤ 58 The ABC's of Coffee
59 Special Coffee Breaks
60 Index
62 Credits
➤ 64 10 Tips for Success:
Guaranteed Perfect Coffee
and Espresso

## *Going Strong*

Coffee is more popular than ever. French bistros, Italian coffee bars, and American coffee shops are exposing us to whole new worlds of flavor. All it takes is a frothy cappuccino and the day is rescued; a demitasse of Melange with a piece of Sachertorte almost makes you feel like you're in Vienna.

A good cup of coffee brightens an otherwise gray day, and the right recipes can bring the espresso bar right into your own home. Have fun taking our little tour of the world of coffee!

# Everything You Need to Know

### Coffee— A Hot Commodity

For many people, that first cup of coffee in the morning is the only way to start the day. But coffee has also become a vital part of the rest of the day—as an aid to digestion after meals, as a pick-me-up at work, or simply as a special treat at the end of a shopping trip. Coffee is equally revered in every country, but the ways in which it is enjoyed are often completely different. In the past few years, typical Italian cafés, cool American coffee shops, and cozy Viennese coffee houses have spread their coffee culture and established a cult around this everyday beverage.

Coffee trees produce flowers and fruit simultaneously.

### Its Origin

Coffee probably originated in Abyssinia (now Ethiopia) and presumably takes its name from the Kaffa province there. Coffee cultivation moved from Africa to Yemen, which soon supplied coffee to the entire Arab world. At the beginning of the 17th century, the first coffee beans were brought to Italy from the Yemeni port city of Mocha. With the siege of Vienna by the Turks in 1683, coffee began its triumphal march through all of Europe. When the Turks retreated, they left behind hundreds of sacks of coffee. A clever Viennese took advantage of the opportunity and immediately opened the city's first coffee house. At first, coffee was rare and expensive, and was therefore reserved for the aristocracy. To meet the large demand, colonial powers established plantations in all suitable, subtropical areas. But coffee didn't become a drink for the common people until the arrival of the new

2 "Coffee beans" are actually the seeds of a cherry-like stone fruit that grows on the coffee tree.

industrial age, when the methods for processing coffee were simplified and the luxury drink became slightly more attainable.

### Coffee Cultivation Today

Today, coffee is mainly grown in the "coffee belt" along the 28th parallel, where ideal conditions for coffee growing prevail: A hot and humid climate with a constant temperature from 17 to 23°C, without the danger of frost even at high altitudes. The world's largest coffee producers are currently Brazil, Colombia, and Indonesia.

## Coffee Plants

Two varieties of coffee plant have endured through the ages and are the most commonly available today: Coffea Arabica and Coffea Robusta. Arabica coffee is less acidic, contains less caffeine, and has a finer, sweetish flavor. It thrives in altitudes from 2600 to 6500 feet, but is unfortunately highly susceptible to pests and frost. Robusta plants, as their name implies, are more resilient but only grow at altitudes from 980 to 2600 feet. Robusta coffee is more bitter, more acidic, has less aroma, and more caffeine than Arabica.

3 *The specific coffee aroma doesn't develop until the beans are roasted.*

## Coffee Processing

Coffee beans are actually the seeds of a cherry-like fruit that grows on the coffee tree. Each fruit contains two seeds enclosed in a parchment skin that must be removed. There are two methods for removing the skin: The "dry" method, in which whole fruits are dried until the beans can be hulled; and the more complex "wet" method, in which the beans are squeezed out of the hulls in a washing process and then re-washed and dried. The practically colorless and odorless coffee beans must then be roasted. This is where each variety takes on its own specific flavor and aroma. The difference is in the temperature and duration of roasting. For example, espresso beans are roasted the longest.

## Preparation

The basic principle is always the same: Hot water is poured over the roasted and ground beans. But at this point, minute differences enter into the picture, starting with the type of grind. Coffee always tastes best when freshly ground. It should not be stored for very long and only in tightly sealed containers. A medium grind is used for normal filter coffee; Turkish coffee requires a powdery grind; whereas, Italian espresso is slightly coarser. Whether you prepare your ground coffee using a manual filter, French press or stove top espresso maker, with the Turkish method or a machine, depends on your particular tastes. The following pages describe the individual methods, although these can be altered as desired.

# The Right Way to Make Coffee

The pros naturally swear by their espresso machines. But you can also prepare good coffee without all the expense. What matters most is the quality of the coffee and the proportions. The following basic principles apply:

➤ For one 6-ounce cup of coffee:
Use ¾ cup water with 2 tbs ground coffee (preferably fresh ground).

➤ For 1 cup espresso:
Use ⅓ cup water with 2 tbs coffee ground for espresso. The exact amounts depend on your tastes, the grind of the coffee, and the pressure of the coffee maker.

## 1 Espresso Machines

Great for those who drink a lot of coffee. The operating systems vary depending on the manufacturer. When you purchase a machine, make sure it creates a high enough pressure and has a steam wand for frothing milk.

## 2 Stove Top Makers & French Presses

Inexpensive and suitable for any household, neither one requires paper filters and both produce aromatic coffee fast. They are available in different sizes and models and can be purchased at most stores.

## 3 Milk Frother

Use it to froth hot milk for cappuccinos, latte macchiatos, etc. Simply pump the built-in plunger up and down several times at a brisk pace to incorporate air into the milk.

## 4 Hand-Held Frother

This small, battery-operated appliance with a miniature whisk head requires less physical effort on your part when frothing milk. It's also great for making milkshakes and mixed drinks as well as for salad dressings.

**TIP** For the recipes in this book, the proportions stated above apply unless otherwise indicated. **"Double-strength coffee"** means twice the amount of coffee to the same amount of water, i.e. instead of 2 tbs coffee, use 4 tbs coffee for ¾ cup water.

# Four International Classics

### Turkish Coffee

Place about $1/2$ cup cold water and 2 tsp sugar in a small pot or Turkish "cezve" (a small brass pot with a narrow top and a long handle), and stir. Add 2 heaping tsp finely ground coffee (or Turkish coffee) and heat while stirring (a light foam should form on the surface). As soon as the coffee begins to bubble up, pour $1/3$ into a cup. Repeat the procedure and then pour the rest of the coffee into the cup. Now just let the coffee grounds settle and drink it while it's hot.

### Cappuccino

Cappuccino is made from equal amounts of espresso and foamed milk. You need 1 cup of freshly brewed espresso (see page 8) and about $1/3$ cup milk (low-fat is best because whole milk hides the coffee aroma). The best foam is made with the steam wand of an espresso machine. Otherwise, you can heat milk in a saucepan and then process it with a milk frother or wire whisk. Immediately pour the milk onto the espresso and, if desired, sprinkle with cocoa.

### Café au lait

For this French morning beverage, equal amounts of coffee and milk are poured into a typical drinking bowl. The recommended method of preparation is with a French press. Pour $3/4$ cup boiling water onto 2 tbs dark roast coffee and let brew for 3–5 minutes, and press down on the filter plunger. Heat, but do not boil $3/4$ cup milk. Pour coffee and milk into the bowl simultaneously. For even more aroma, add a little chicory or wheat coffee to the ground coffee.

### Viennese Melange

This is simply a mixture of coffee and hot milk. The color of the melange as determined by the amount of milk was practically a topic of philosophical debate in Vienna as each coffee house has its own recipe. Basically, however, it's made by brewing coffee from $3/4$ cup water and 2 tbs dark roast coffee or espresso. Pour into a cup and add about $3/4$ cup hot (not boiling) milk.

# Making Espresso

The Italians simply call their espresso "caffè" and actually it doesn't matter, if you prepare it with a professional machine or the traditional stovetop maker. Espresso is the essence of coffee and the basis for many drinks, such as cappuccino and latte macchiato. Espresso is famous for being small, strong, and black. It's okay to sweeten it with sugar, but milk is frowned upon.

All you need to make the basic espresso recipe is espresso coffee (preferably freshly ground) of a little darker roast than normal filter coffee (in this case, Arabica is ideal) and really hot water.

## Espresso from a Stove Top Maker

MAKES 1 OR 2 SERVINGS

➤ **2 tbs ground espresso coffee**
**$^1/_3$–$^1/_2$ cup spring water or bottled water**
**Sugar (optional)**

**1** Unscrew espresso maker and pour in the right amount of water (do not cover valve).

**2** Place one spoonful of ground coffee in the filter basket per cup and spread smooth – don't tamp it down. Then insert the basket in the lower section of the pot.

**3** Heat pot on the stove at the highest setting. As soon as espresso starts to hiss in the tube, remove from heat.

**4** Stir finished espresso once in the pot and then pour it into cups (preferably use prewarmed). If desired, add sugar.

# Flavoring Coffee

## Caramel Syrup

To make approximately ⅞ cup syrup, pour 1 cup sugar into a saucepan and caramelize over medium heat until melted and golden brown. Carefully pour in 1 cup water. Reheat hardened caramel to loosen it from the bottom of the pan and simmer over low heat for about 10 minutes. Transfer syrup to bottles and seal. Keeps in the refrigerator for about 1 year.

➤ Vanilla Syrup: When adding water to the sugar, also add pulp scraped from a vanilla bean and the bean itself. Remove bean from finished syrup.

➤ Almond Syrup: Add 1 tsp almond extract and 1 tbs Amaretto (optional) to the finished caramel syrup.

## Fruit Syrup

To make 1¾ cups syrup, combine 1 cup sugar and 2 cups fruit juice (such as cherry, currant, or freshly squeezed orange juice) in a sauce pan, and stir well. Simmer uncovered over medium heat for 10–15 minutes until the liquid becomes more syrupy. Transfer finished syrup to a bottle and store in the refrigerator. Keeps for about 1 year.

➤ You can also flavor the syrup with spices such as a pinch of cinnamon, cloves or ginger, or with a little grated lemon or orange zest. Simply simmer the spices along with the juice. If you use lemon or orange zest, pour the syrup into a strainer.

## Coffee Syrup

To make about 1 cup syrup, combine 1 cup sugar and ½ cup water in a saucepan. Stir to dissolve sugar and boil over high heat while stirring constantly for about 5 minutes. Add ⅞ cup strong, freshly brewed espresso and immediately remove from heat. Transfer finished syrup to a bottle and store in a refrigerator. Keeps for about 1 year.

➤ You can also flavor the syrup with 1 pinch cardamom, cinnamon or cloves, or 1–2 tbs cognac or orange liqueur. It's very good in milkshakes and is especially delicious as a topping on ice cream and desserts.

## Other Things that Go with Coffee

➤ Spices: Add some cardamom, cinnamon, cloves, ginger, or a little grated orange zest to the ground coffee before brewing, or stir into the finished coffee and let stand briefly.

➤ Brandies and Liqueurs: Simply stir such classics as fruit brandies, grappa, or cognac into the finished coffee. Or add amaretto, advocaat, or orange-, coffee-, or chocolate-flavored liqueurs. Another fancy twist is to whip cream together with the alcohol or syrup, and use it to top the coffee.

➤ Cream and Ice Cream: Plain whipped cream or whipped cream sweetened, sprinkled with grated chocolate or cookie crumbs, or flavored with spices or alcohol is a suitable adornment to any cup of coffee. Vanilla, chocolate, mocha, and nut-flavored ice creams are especially good in hot coffee as well as in ice cream coffee.

9

# Just Coffee

Do you want cream or sugar with that? It's a crime to limit coffee to this simple combination, when it's so easy to liven it up with spices, syrups, or liqueurs, mix it with ice cream or crown it with whipped cream. The possibilities range from such classics as Irish Coffee and Ice Cream Coffee to totally new creations like Mandarin-Orange Mocha Smoothies and Herbal Coffee Cocktails.

11  Swiss Plum Coffee
11  Ice Cream Coffee
13  Almond Coffee
13  Latte Macchiato
15  Black Forest Cherry Coffee
15  After Eight Mint Coffee
15  Viennese Chocolate Coffee
16  Mexican Coffee
16  Ginger Coffee
16  Spanish Coffee
19  Café Brulôt
19  Irish Coffee
19  Brandy and Chocolate Coffee
21  White Chocolate Latte

21  Kaiser Melange
21  Coffee Nog
23  Mandarin-Orange Mocha Smoothie
23  Cool Cocoa-Coconut
23  Banana Coffee Shake
24  Advocaat Ice Cream Coffee
24  Marzipan Coffee
24  Mocha Latte on the Rocks
27  Herbal Coffee Cocktail
27  Hot Coffee Shot
27  Mocha Brandy Cocktail
27  Mocha Flip

# Quick Recipes

## Swiss Plum Coffee

MAKES 2 SERVINGS

➤ 3 tbs plum butter | 3 tbs plum brandy (optional) | 1 pinch cloves | $1/4$ cup heavy cream | 1 tsp sugar | $1^1/4$ cups hot coffee | Cocoa powder | Cinnamon for garnish

1 | In a saucepan, combine plum butter, 2 tbs plum brandy (may substitute water), and cloves. Stir until smooth and heat over low heat.

2 | Whip cream, sugar, and remaining plum brandy, if desired, just until very softly whipped.

3 | Pour coffee into the plum butter and add cocoa powder. Stir thoroughly with a wire whisk and pour into 2 cups. Top with whipped cream, stir a little, and sprinkle with cinnamon.

## Ice Cream Coffee

MAKES 2 SERVINGS

➤ $1/2$ cup heavy cream | 2 tsp sugar | $1/2$ tsp vanilla extract | 2 scoops vanilla ice cream | $1^1/4$ cups coffee, chilled | Chocolate shavings for garnish

1 | Whip cream with sugar and vanilla until stiff. Distribute vanilla ice cream in 2 glasses or sundae glasses and pour coffee over the top.

2 | Spoon whipped cream onto coffee or pipe on with a pastry bag, and sprinkle with chocolate shavings. If desired, flavor the coffee with syrup (such as caramel or vanilla syrup) or drizzle a little chocolate liqueur over the whipped cream.

Smooth | Mild
# Almond Coffee

MAKES 2 SERVINGS

➤ 7/8 cup low-fat milk
2 tbs almond butter (from a jar)
1 pinch cinnamon
7/8 cup hot coffee
2 tbs Amaretto (optional)
1 tbs almond syrup

🕐 Prep time: 10 minutes
🕐 Cooling time: 2 hours
➤ Calories/serving: About 160

1 | In a saucepan, combine milk, almond butter, and cinnamon and stir well. Heat while stirring but do not boil. Remove from heat and let stand for 2 hours.

2 | Reheat almond milk. Stir in coffee, amaretto, and almond syrup. Foam with a blender and transfer to 2 large glasses.

Italian Classic
# Latte Macchiato

MAKES 2 SERVINGS

➤ 1 3/4 cups low-fat milk
2/3 cup hot espresso
4 tsp sugar (optional)
Cocoa powder for garnish

🕐 Prep time: 10 minutes
➤ Calories/serving: About 120

1 | In a saucepan, heat milk but do not boil. Foam thoroughly with a blender or milk frother.

2 | Sweeten espresso with sugar as desired. Pour hot milk into 2 tall glasses. Slowly let espresso run down into the milk over the back of a teaspoon and down one side of the glass (this will produce 2 decorative layers). If you want, dust the milk with a little cocoa. Serve Latte Macchiato immediately.

**TIPS**

You can also vary Latte Macchiato by using different flavors of milk:

➤ Heat milk with the pulp scraped out of 1 vanilla bean, the bean itself, and 1 tsp vanilla extract. Remove from heat, let stand for 2 hours. Reheat and remove vanilla bean, and then foam.

➤ Heat milk with 5 cardamom pods that have been slit open, 1 cinnamon stick, and 2 tbs honey. Remove from heat, let stand for 2 hours. Reheat and pour milk through a strainer, and then foam.

➤ Or simply flavor the milk with syrups such as almond or caramel or with commercial syrups.

### Fruity

# Black Forest Cherry Coffee

MAKES 2 SERVINGS

➤ 1/4 cup heavy cream

  1 tsp cocoa powder

  7/8 cup milk

  1/3 cup semisweet chocolate chips

  2 tsp cherry brandy (optional)

  6 tbs cherry syrup

  1 cup hot, strong coffee

  Chocolate shavings and maraschino cherries

🕐 Prep time: 15 minutes

➤ Calories/serving: About 415

1 | Whip cream until stiff. Stir cocoa powder into 3 tbs cold milk. Heat remaining milk. Add chocolate chips and stir over medium heat until melted. Stir in cocoa mixture.

2 | Pour cherry brandy and 4 tbs cherry syrup into 2 cups. Combine chocolate milk and coffee, pour into cups, and stir. Top each cup with a little whipped cream, several cherries, remaining syrup, and grated chocolate.

### Unusual

# After Eight Mint Coffee

MAKES 2 SERVINGS

➤ 1/4 cup heavy cream

  3 tbs sugar, divided use

  2 tsp cocoa powder

  1/2 cup milk

  7/8 cup hot coffee

  4 tbs peppermint syrup (Italian-style syrup for sodas)

  4 After Eight mints

  Fresh mint leaves for garnish

🕐 Prep time: 10 minutes

➤ Calories/serving: About 340

1 | Whip cream with 1 tsp sugar until stiff. Stir remaining sugar and cocoa powder into 3 tbs of the cold milk. Bring remaining milk to a boil and stir in cocoa-milk mixture.

2 | Combine cocoa mixture, coffee, and 3 tbs peppermint syrup. Pour into 2 cups and top each with a dollop of whipped cream. Cut After Eight mints in half diagonally and stick into the whipped cream. Drizzle remaining peppermint syrup over the coffee and garnish with mint leaves.

### Full-Bodied

# Viennese Chocolate Coffee

MAKES 2 SERVINGS

➤ 1/2 cup semisweet chocolate chips

  1/2 cup heavy cream, divided use

  1 pinch cinnamon

  1 pinch cardamom

  1 1/2 cups hot coffee

  1 tbs honey

  1 tsp sugar

  Cinnamon and cardamom for garnish

🕐 Prep time: 10 minutes

➤ Calories/serving: About 375

1 | In a small saucepan, stir semisweet chocolate over very low heat until melted. Using a wire whisk, thoroughly mix 1/4 cup of the cream, cinnamon, and cardamom into the chocolate. Sweeten coffee with honey and add to chocolate. Stir well with a wire whisk.

2 | Whip remaining 1/4 cup cream with sugar until stiff. Pour coffee mixture into 2 cups and top with whipped cream. Sprinkle with cinnamon and cardamom.

◄ *Photo top:* **Black Forest Cherry Coffee** *Photo middle:* **After Eight Mint Coffee**
*Photo bottom:* **Viennese Chocolate Coffee**

Spicy | Fancy
# Mexican Coffee
MAKES 2 SERVINGS

- ➤ 1 dried chile pepper
  3 cinnamon sticks
  $1/4$ cup brown sugar
  2 tbs ground espresso
  2 pieces semisweet chocolate (about $1/2$ oz each)
  2 tbs coffee liqueur (optional)

🕐 Prep time: 20 minutes
➤ Calories/serving: About 150

1 | Slit open chile pepper and place in a saucepan with 1 cinnamon stick and brown sugar. Add $1/4$ cup water and boil over high heat for about 5 minutes until sugar is slightly thickened and caramelized to a golden brown color.

2 | Add $1\frac{3}{4}$ cups water to the sugar syrup. Add coffee, bring to a boil, and remove from heat. Cover and let stand for 5 minutes.

3 | Place 1 piece of chocolate in each of 2 cups. Strain coffee into the cups. Add liqueur, if desired. Stir each cup with 1 cinnamon stick and serve.

Zesty | Warms You Up
# Ginger Coffee
MAKES 2 SERVINGS

- ➤ 1 piece fresh ginger (about 1 in)
  1 orange
  $1/2$ cup sugar
  4 cloves
  2 star anise
  1 cinnamon stick
  $1/3$ cup heavy cream
  $1\frac{3}{4}$ cups hot, strong espresso
  Chopped pistachios for garnish

🕐 Prep time: 25 minutes
➤ Calories/serving: About 345

1 | Peel ginger and slice. Grate 1 tsp zest from the orange and squeeze juice; set aside. In a small saucepan heat ginger, half the orange zest, sugar, and spices over low heat until golden and caramelized. Carefully pour in $1/2$ cup water and orange juice, and simmer for about 15 minutes until syrupy. Remove from heat and let cool.

2 | Whip cream until stiff. Strain half the syrup into 2 cups and add espresso. Spoon on whipped cream and top with remaining syrup, orange zest, and pistachios.

Fruity | Warms You Up
# Spanish Coffee
MAKES 2 SERVINGS

- ➤ 1 orange
  4 whole cloves
  6 tbs heavy cream
  3 tbs sugar
  4 tbs cream sherry
  $1\frac{1}{4}$ cups hot, strong coffee
  1 tsp cocoa powder

🕐 Prep time: 15 minutes
➤ Calories/serving: About 240

1 | Cut 2 slices from the center of the orange and pierce each slice with 2 cloves. Grate zest from 1 orange half. Squeeze juice from both remaining halves. Whip cream until stiff.

2 | In a small saucepan heat sugar and orange slices until caramelized to a light-brown color. Pour in orange juice and simmer for 2-3 minutes. Remove from heat and stir in sherry. Combine coffee and cocoa. Place 1 orange slice and half the orange syrup in each of 2 cups. Add coffee, top with whipped cream, and sprinkle with grated orange zest.

## Classic
# Café Brulôt

MAKES 2 SERVINGS

➤ 3 tbs cognac

4 tsp orange liqueur (e.g., Cointreau)

2 whole cloves

1 cinnamon stick

Zest stripped from half an orange

Zest stripped from half a lemon

4 tsp sugar

1 cup hot, strong coffee

Whipped cream (optional)

🕐 Prep time: 10 minutes

➤ Calories/serving: About 120

1 | In a saucepan, warm cognac, orange liqueur, cloves, cinnamon stick, orange zest, lemon zest, and sugar. Stir until sugar is dissolved.

2 | Carefully light the spice-alcohol mixture with a match. As the flame starts to go out, add coffee slowly and carefully. Strain into cups. Serve with whipped cream, if desired.

## Classic
# Irish Coffee

MAKES 2 SERVINGS

➤ 1/3 cup heavy cream

1 3/4 cups hot, strong coffee

5 tbs Irish whiskey

2 tsp brown sugar

1 tsp cocoa powder

Irish coffee glasses

🕐 Prep time: 10 minutes

➤ Calories/serving: About 230

1 | Prewarm 2 glasses by filling them with hot water. Whip cream just until softly whipped.

2 | Pour water out of the glasses. Divide coffee, whiskey, and sugar between the 2 glasses. Stir until sugar is dissolved. Top with whipped cream and dust with cocoa powder.

**TIP** Special warmers are available for Irish coffee. The glass is suspended in a stand above a flame and you heat the coffee by rotating the glass.

## Classic
# Brandy and Chocolate Coffee

MAKES 2 SERVINGS

➤ 1/4 cup heavy cream

1 tsp granulated sugar

1/4 tsp vanilla extract

6 sugar cubes

1/2 cup brandy

1 1/4 cups hot coffee

2 tsp chocolate shavings

2 tall coffee mugs

🕐 Prep time: 15 minutes

➤ Calories/serving: About 260

1 | Whip cream with sugar and vanilla until stiff. Place 3 sugar cubes in each mug.

2 | Heat brandy in a saucepan. Pour half the brandy over the sugar in each cup and light with a match. As soon as the flame goes out, carefully pour in the coffee.

3 | Top coffee with whipped cream and chocolate shavings.

◀ *Photo top:* **Café Brulôt**    *Photo middle:* **Irish Coffee**    *Photo bottom:* **Brandy and Chocolate Coffee**

Creamy | Mild
# White Chocolate Latte

MAKES 2 SERVINGS

➤ ¹/₂ cup white chocolate baking chips or 3 oz white chocolate

1¹/₄ cups milk

1 vanilla bean

1 tbs maple syrup

¹/₂ cup hot espresso

2 tbs espresso syrup (may substitute chocolate sauce)

Chocolate shavings for garnish

⏱ Prep time: 10 minutes
➤ Calories/serving: About 385

1 | In a saucepan, combine white chocolate and milk. Slit open vanilla bean, scrape out pulp, and add bean and pulp to the milk.

2 | Stir chocolate mixture over low heat until melted. Stir in maple syrup and remove from heat. Remove vanilla bean, foam chocolate milk, and pour into glasses.

3 | Combine espresso and syrup. Pour over milk in a zigzag pattern. Sprinkle with chocolate shavings.

**TIP**
A chocolate latte is also delicious cold. Let milk and coffee cool. Foam cold milk and transfer to glasses along with 2 scoops chocolate or mocha ice cream per glass. Pour coffee over the top and garnish with chocolate shavings.

Classic
# Kaiser Melange

MAKES 2 SERVINGS

➤ ¹/₄ cup heavy cream

2 pasteurized egg yolks* or 2 tbs pasteurized whole eggs

2 tsp sugar

1 cup hot, strong coffee

4 tsp cognac (optional)

⏱ Prep time: 10 minutes
➤ Calories/serving: About 195

1 | Using a wire whisk, beat cream, egg yolks, and sugar until foamy.

2 | Pour egg mixture into 2 cups. Combine coffee with cognac, if desired, and pour onto the egg mixture.

* Note: Raw egg yolks should be consumed with caution. Not recommended for children, elderly, or health compromised individuals.

Satisfying | Smooth
# Coffee Nog

MAKES 2 SERVINGS

➤ 1³/₄ cups milk

2 egg yolks

1 tsp sugar

1 tsp vanilla extract

¹/₃ cup strong espresso

3 tbs whiskey

2 tbs rum

Freshly grated nutmeg

⏱ Prep time: 15 minutes
➤ Calories/serving: About 325

1 | Heat milk in a saucepan. Using a hand mixer or wire whisk, beat egg yolks, sugar, and vanilla extract until mixture is a light-yellow color.

2 | Gradually stir egg yolks into milk. Heat over low heat just to 160°F, stirring constantly. Do not boil. Then stir in espresso, whiskey, and rum. Immediately pour into 2 large mugs and garnish with nutmeg.

Fruity | As Dessert

# Mandarin-Orange Mocha Smoothie

MAKES 2 SERVINGS

- ➤ 3 mandarin oranges
- 1/2 cup cold, strong espresso
- 1/2 cup plain yogurt
- 1/3 cup milk
- 2–3 tbs sugar
- 2 tbs orange liqueur (optional)
- 1 tsp vanilla extract
- 4 ice cubes
- Spiral strips of mandarin orange zest
- Chocolate shavings for garnish

- ⏱ Prep time: 15 minutes
- ➤ Calories/serving: About 170

1 | Squeeze juice from 1 mandarin orange. Peel remaining oranges, including white membrane, and cut into pieces, saving any juice.

2 | In a blender, purée mandarin pieces, juice, and all remaining ingredients with the ice cubes. Pour into 2 tall glasses. Hang spiral peels on the rims of the glasses and sprinkle chocolate shavings on top.

Refreshing | Exotic

# Cool Cocoa-Coconut Coffee

MAKES 2 SERVINGS

- ➤ 7/8 cup unsweetened coconut milk (canned)
- 3 tbs sugar
- 1/2 tsp cocoa powder
- 1/2 vanilla bean
- 2 tbs coconut liqueur (optional)
- 1 1/4 cups cold coffee
- Ice cubes

- ⏱ Prep time: 15 minutes
- ⏱ Cooling time: 1 hour
- ➤ Calories/serving: About 180

1 | Combine 6 tbs of the coconut milk, sugar, and cocoa. Set aside. Slit open vanilla bean. In a saucepan, bring vanilla bean and remaining coconut milk to a boil. Stir in cocoa mixture. Remove from heat and let cool.

2 | Remove vanilla bean from cocoa-coconut milk. Stir in coconut liqueur, if desired. Using a blender or milk frother, stir until foamy. Place 4–5 ice cubes in each of 2 glasses. Pour in coffee and foamed cocoa-coconut milk.

Suitable for Breakfast

# Banana Coffee Shake

MAKES 2 SERVINGS

- 2 ripe bananas
- 1 tsp lemon juice
- 1 tsp cinnamon, divided use
- 2/3 cup milk
- 2/3 cup plain yogurt
- 1/2 cup vanilla ice cream
- 1/2 cup cold coffee
- 2 tbs maple syrup
- 4 ice cubes

- ⏱ Prep time: 10 minutes
- ➤ Calories/serving: About 215

1 | Peel bananas, cut into pieces, and combine with lemon juice.

2 | Reserve half the cinnamon for garnish. Combine remaining cinnamon, bananas, and all remaining ingredients in a blender with the ice cubes. Purée until foamy.

3 | Immediately pour shake into 2 tall glasses and garnish with remaining cinnamon.

◀ *Photo left:* **Mandarin-Orange Mocha Smoothie**   *Photo middle:* **Cool Cocoa-Coconut Coffee**
*Photo right:* **Banana Coffee Shake**

As Dessert | Creamy
# Advocaat Ice Cream Coffee

MAKES 2 SERVINGS
- ➤ ½ cup heavy cream
- 1 tbs sugar
- 4 large scoops chocolate ice cream
- 1 cup cold coffee
- 3 tbs coffee liqueur
- ¼ cup advocaat
- Advocaat, chocolate sprinkles, and rolled wafer cookies for garnish

- 🕐 Prep time: 10 minutes
- ➤ Calories/serving: About 545

1 | Whip cream with sugar until stiff. Place 1 scoop of chocolate ice cream in each of 2 glasses.

2 | Combine remaining ice cream, coffee, coffee liqueur and advocaat in a blender, and blend at a high speed until foamy.

3 | Pour advocaat coffee over the ice cream. Pipe on whipped cream, using a pastry bag. Drizzle a little advocaat over the whipped cream and garnish with chocolate sprinkles and rolled wafer cookies.

Sophisticated | Easy
# Marzipan Coffee

MAKES 2 SERVINGS
- ➤ ½ cup heavy cream
- 3-4 almond macaroons (or use Amarettini cookies on page 57)
- 3 oz marzipan
- ⅞ cup low-fat milk
- ½ cup cold coffee
- 2 scoops vanilla ice cream

- 🕐 Prep time: 10 minutes
- ➤ Calories/serving: About 440

1 | Whip cream until stiff. Place almond macaroons or Amarettini cookies in a clean plastic bag and crush with a rolling pin. Fold cookie crumbs into whipped cream, setting aside about 1 tbs for garnish.

2 | Cut marzipan into pieces and purée with half the milk until smooth. Add remaining milk, coffee, and ice cream. Purée at high speed until foamy. Pour into glasses. Top with whipped cream and sprinkle with remaining cookie crumbs.

Fancy / Refreshing
# Mocha Latte on the Rocks

MAKES 2 SERVINGS
- ➤ ⅞ cup low-fat milk
- 2 tbs coffee beans
- 2 tbs light-colored honey (e.g., acacia or floral honey)
- ⅞ cup cold espresso

- 🕐 Prep time: 10 minutes
- 🕐 Freezing time: 4 hours
- ➤ Calories/serving: About 65

1 | In a saucepan, heat milk and coffee beans. Just before the milk starts to boil, remove from heat. Stir in honey, cover, and let cool.

2 | Pour espresso into an ice cube tray and freeze for 4 hours.

3 | Using an ice crusher or meat mallet, coarsely crush espresso ice cubes and transfer to 2 glasses. Strain coffee milk over the espresso ice and serve immediately.

*Photo top left:* **Advocaat Ice Cream Coffee** *Photo top right:* **Marzipan Coffee** ➤
*Photo bottom:* **Mocha Latte on the Rocks**

### Herbal | Fancy
# Herbal Coffee Cocktail

MAKES 1 COCKTAIL

➤ 3 tbs green Chartreuse
  (French herbal liqueur)
  2 tbs cold, strong coffee
  2 tbs heavy cream
  2 tsp whiskey
  2 tsp cocoa liqueur
  3 ice cubes
  1 maraschino cherry
  for garnish

🕓 Prep time: 5 minutes
➤ Calories/serving: About 160

1 | Combine all ingredients in a cocktail shaker with the ice cubes and shake vigorously for about 15 seconds.

2 | Strain shaker contents into a glass. Garnish with the maraschino cherry.

### Fancy
# Hot Coffee Shot

MAKES 1 COCKTAIL

2 tbs heavy cream
4 tsp hot espresso
4 tsp Galliano (Italian herb
  and spice liqueur)

🕓 Prep time: 10 minutes
➤ Calories/serving: About 125

1 | Briskly beat cream with a whisk or fork just until it is very softly whipped.

2 | Pour espresso into a tall, narrow glass. Slowly pour Galliano into the glass over the back of a teaspoon so two separate layers are formed. In the same way, slowly pour softly whipped cream onto the Galliano.

### Smooth | Sweet
# Mocha Brandy Cocktail

MAKES 1 COCKTAIL

4 tsp brandy
4 tsp apricot brandy
4 tsp cold, strong coffee
2 tsp advocaat
2 tsp heavy cream
3 ice cubes
Cocoa powder for garnish

Prep time: 5 minutes
Calories/serving: About 145

1 | Combine all ingredients in a cocktail shaker with the ice cubes and shake vigorously for about 15 seconds.

2 | Strain shaker contents into a glass. Garnish with a little cocoa powder.

### Classic
# Mocha Flip

MAKES 1 COCKTAIL

➤ 1/2 cup milk
  3 tbs cold, strong espresso
  3 tbs brandy
  1 tbs coffee liqueur
  1 tsp powdered sugar
  1 tsp cocoa powder
  1 fresh egg yolk or 1 tbs
  pasteurized egg product*
  1 pinch cloves
  4 ice cubes

🕓 Prep time: 5 minutes
➤ Calories/serving: About 300

1 | Combine all ingredients in a cocktail shaker with the ice cubes and shake vigorously for about 15 seconds.

2 | Strain shaker contents into a glass.

* Note: Raw egg yolks should be consumed with caution. Not recommended for children, elderly, or health compromised individuals.

◀ *Photo top left:* **Herbal Coffee Cocktail**    *Photo top right:* **Hot Coffee Shot**
*Photo bottom left:* **Mocha Brandy Cocktail**    *Photo bottom right:* **Mocha Flip**

27

# Made with Coffee

If you only know coffee as a beverage, you've really missed out. Its powerful aroma is also fantastic for flavoring desserts, baked goods, and candy. When a cup of coffee is accompanied by Mocha Truffles or a piece of Mocha Layer Cake, it doubles your pleasure!

29   Coconut Coffee Toffees

29   Espresso Cream
     with Raspberries

31   Mocha Parfait

31   Spiced Coffee Granita

33   Caffè Cotta

33   Tiramisu

34   Mousse au Café

34   Coffee Flan

37   Mocha Soufflé with
     Orange Compote

39   Milk-and-Coffee Zabaglione

39   Mocha Truffles

41   Amaretti Cake

41   Mocha Layer Cake

# Quick Recipes

## Coconut Coffee Toffees

MAKES ABOUT 50 TOFFEES

➤ 5 tbs butter │ 2 tbs instant coffee │
½ cup sugar │ 5 tbs light-colored honey
(e.g., acacia or floral honey) │ ¾ cup
sweetened flaked coconut │ Vegetable
oil for the pan

1 │ Cut butter into bits and place in the
freezer. Dissolve instant coffee in 3 tbs
hot water.

2 │ In a saucepan, stir sugar and honey
until the mixture is golden and
caramelized. Remove pan from heat.
Gradually add butter, stirring well. Stir
in coffee and grated coconut. Brush a
4 x 8-inch loaf pan with oil. Pour in
mixture, let harden, and cut into
1-inch squares.

## Espresso Cream with Raspberries

MAKES 4 SERVINGS

➤ 3 oz coffee-flavored chocolate or bitter-
sweet chocolate │ 8 oz mascarpone │
8 oz low-fat cream cheese │ 5 tbs sugar │
1 tsp vanilla extract │ ¼ cup cold,
strong espresso │ 3 cups fresh raspberries │ ¼ cup coffee liqueur (optional) │
Mint leaves for garnish

1 │ Chop chocolate and melt in a double
boiler. Let cool slightly.

2 │ Meanwhile, in a medium bowl combine
mascarpone, cream cheese, sugar, vanilla,
and espresso. Stir in melted chocolate. In
a small serving bowl, alternate layers of
cheese mixture and raspberries. Drizzle
with coffee liqueur if desired, and garnish
with mint leaves.

29

## For Special Occasions
# Mocha Parfait

MAKES ONE 8- OR 9-INCH
LOAF PAN (12 SLICES)

- 1 cup dried plums
- 1/3 cup Armagnac (may substitute plum juice)
- 4 egg yolks
- 3/4 cup powdered sugar
- 6 tbs double-strength espresso
- 1/2 tsp cinnamon
- 3 egg whites
- 7/8 cup heavy cream
- Plastic wrap for the pan

- Prep time: 35 minutes
- Marinating time: 4 hours
- Freezing time: 12 hours
- Calories/serving: About 120

1 | Cut plums into quarters and soak in Armagnac for 4 hours.

2 | Place egg yolks in a bowl suspended over lightly boiling water. Add powdered sugar and beat with the whisk attachment of a hand blender for about 7 minutes until thick and creamy. Mix in espresso and cinnamon. Remove bowl from double boiler and continue stirring for another 7 minutes as it cools.

3 | Using a hand mixer, beat egg whites and cream in separate bowls until stiff. Carefully fold both into the egg yolk-coffee mixture and then fold in the plums with the Armagnac. Pour this mixture into a loaf pan lined with plastic wrap and freeze overnight. Remove from the pan, slice, and serve frozen.

## Can Prepare in Advance
# Spiced Coffee Granita

MAKES 4 SERVINGS

- 3 cardamom pods
- 2 whole cloves
- 1 cinnamon stick
- Zest from half an orange
- 1/2 cup sugar
- 1 cup strong espresso
- 1/2 cup heavy cream
- 4 tbs coffee liqueur (optional)
- Chocolate-covered espresso beans for garnish

- Prep time: 10 minutes
- Cooling and freezing time: 3 hours and 30 minutes
- Calories/serving: About 285

1 | Slit open cardamom pods lengthwise. In a saucepan, combine cardamom pods, cloves, cinnamon stick, orange zest, sugar, and 1/2 cup water. Boil for 5 minutes. Remove from heat, add espresso, cover, and let cool for about 1 hour.

2 | Strain coffee into a shallow metal or plastic bowl and place in the freezer. After about 20 minutes, stir with a fork and push the ice crystals away from the edges and into the center. Repeat this procedure about every 20 minutes for a total of 2 hours until all the liquid is frozen into ice crystals.

3 | Whip cream just until softly whipped. Spoon Granita into 4 tall, chilled glasses. Top each with a dollop of heavy cream. Drizzle with coffee liqueur if desired, and garnish with chocolate-covered espresso beans.

### Inexpensive
# Caffè Cotta

MAKES 4 SERVINGS

- 4 molds or soufflé cups (each holding about $2/3$ cup)

  1 pkg unflavored gelatin (about $1/4$ oz)

  2 cups heavy cream

  $1/2$ cup double-strength espresso

  5 tbs sugar

  Pulp scraped from 1 vanilla bean

  2 tbs cognac (optional)

🕐 Prep time: 25 minutes

🕐 Refrigeration time: 4 hours

➤ Calories/serving: About 380

1 | Place empty molds in the refrigerator to chill. Soften gelatin in $1/3$ cup cold water for 10 minutes. In the meantime, combine cream, espresso, sugar, and vanilla pulp in a saucepan.

2 | Bring cream to a boil, add cognac, if desired, and remove from heat. Using a wire whisk, stir gelatin into hot cream. Pour coffee cream into chilled molds and refrigerate for about 4 hours.

3 | Carefully loosen Caffè Cotta cream from the sides of the molds with the tip of a sharp knife. Invert molds onto plates.

**TIP** If you want, you can also pour the Caffè Cotta cream into glass cups and serve with whipped cream on the top.

### Italian Classic
# Tiramisu

MAKES 6 SERVINGS

- 1 cup cold espresso

  6 tbs amaretto

  4 egg yolks

  $1/4$ cup sugar

  16 oz mascarpone

  8 oz ladyfingers

  Cocoa powder for garnish

🕐 Prep time: 20 minutes

🕐 Refrigeration time: 5 hours

➤ Calories/serving: About 645

1 | Combine espresso and amaretto. Using a hand mixer or wire whisk, beat egg yolks and sugar until smooth and the mixture turns light-yellow and thick. Stir in mascarpone one spoonful at a time.

2 | Arrange half the ladyfingers in a rectangular pan and drench with half the espresso-amaretto mixture. Spoon on half the mascarpone cream and smooth out the surface. Top with remaining ladyfingers and drench with remaining coffee mixture. Spread with remaining mascarpone cream and smooth out the surface.

3 | Cover and refrigerate for 4–5 hours. Just before serving, dust with a thick layer of cocoa powder.

**TIP** Be sure to use very fresh eggs. If you're worried about salmonella and want to avoid eggs altogether, here's an alternative cream:

Instead of eggs, combine mascarpone with $2/3$ cup plain or vanilla yogurt and $1/2$ cup advocaat, and stir until smooth.

## Classic
# Mousse au Café

MAKES 6 SERVINGS

- ➤ 1$\frac{1}{4}$ cups semisweet chocolate chips
  3 tbs butter
  6 eggs, separated*
  3 tbs powdered sugar
  2 tbs instant coffee
  $\frac{1}{2}$ tsp grated orange zest
  1 pinch cardamom
  2 tsp coffee liqueur (may substitute strong coffee)
  White chocolate shavings for garnish
  Strips of orange zest for garnish

- 🕐 Prep time. 35 minutes
- 🕐 Refrigeration time: 6 hours
- ➤ Calories/serving: About 260

1 | Melt chocolate in a double boiler. Melt butter in a pan. Beat egg whites with 1 tbs powdered sugar until stiff.

2 | Combine egg yolks, remaining sugar, instant coffee, orange zest and cardamom, and beat until foamy. Gradually stir in melted chocolate and then melted butter. Stir in coffee liqueur. Carefully fold in beaten egg whites.

3 | Pour mousse into a bowl, cover, and refrigerate for about 6 hours. Garnish servings with chocolate shavings and orange zest.

## Can Prepare in Advance
# Coffee Flan

MAKES 6 SERVINGS

- ➤ 1$\frac{1}{4}$ cups sugar, divided use
  3 tbs coffee beans, divided use
  3 tbs cognac (may substitute freshly squeezed orange juice)
  $\frac{1}{2}$ vanilla bean
  1$\frac{3}{4}$ cups milk
  $\frac{1}{2}$ cup heavy cream
  4 eggs
  6 individual baking dishes (each holding about $\frac{2}{3}$ cup)

- 🕐 Prep time: 1 hour and 15 minutes
- 🕐 Refrigeration time: 6 hours
- ➤ Calories/serving: About 300

1 | In a saucepan, caramelize $\frac{3}{4}$ cup of the sugar until light-brown. Pour half the caramel into the baking dishes and mix the rest with $\frac{1}{2}$ cup water. Add 1 tbs coffee beans to the saucepan and boil hard for about 5 minutes (the caramel should be liquid). Add cognac, bring to a boil briefly, and set aside.

2 | Fill a deep baking dish with about 1-inch of water and place in the oven (middle rack). Preheat oven to 325°F. Slit open vanilla bean and heat along with remaining coffee beans, milk, and cream. Using a hand mixer, beat eggs and remaining sugar until creamy. Pour warm milk through a strainer and stir into egg cream. Pour this mixture into the baking dishes.

3 | Place baking dishes in the water in the oven and bake for about 40 minutes until firm. Remove dishes from water and refrigerate for 6 hours. Loosen cream from the sides of the dishes with a sharp knife and invert onto plates. Pour remaining coffee caramel with coffee beans over the top and serve.

*Note: Raw egg yolks should be consumed with caution. Not recommended for children, elderly, or health compromised individuals.

*Photo top:* **Mousse au Café**   *Photo bottom:* **Coffee Flan** ➤

For Special Occasions

# Mocha Soufflé with Orange Compote

MAKES 8 RAMEKINS

➤ **For the compote:**

**5 oranges**

**3 tbs sugar**

**2 tbs orange liqueur (optional)**

**1 dash cinnamon**

➤ **For the soufflé:**

**½ cup flour**

**½ cup sugar, divided use**

**1 tsp cocoa powder**

**1 pinch cloves**

**½ cup strong coffee**

**3 eggs, separated**

**3 oz cream cheese**

**2 tbs coffee liqueur (optional)**

**Butter for the ramekins**

**3 tbs bread crumbs**

🕐 Prep time: 45 minutes

🕐 Baking time: 30 minutes

➤ Calories/serving: About 185

**1** | For the compote, peel 4 oranges with a sharp knife so that no white membrane remains, and cut segments away from inner membranes, saving any juice. Squeeze juice from remaining orange.

**2** | In a saucepan, heat sugar until light-brown and caramelized. Pour in orange juice and reduce by half over high heat. Flavor to taste with orange liqueur and cinnamon. Fold in orange segments and set aside to cool.

**3** | For the soufflé, combine flour, ¼ cup sugar, cocoa, and cloves. Pour in coffee, stir well, and bring to a boil while stirring constantly (1).

Remove from heat and let cool. Stir cream cheese and liqueur into the cooled coffee mixture. Thoroughly stir in egg yolks one at a time.

**4** | Preheat the oven to 400°F. Beat egg whites with remaining ¼ cup sugar until stiff. Carefully fold egg whites into batter (2).

**5** | Grease ramekins and coat with bread crumbs (3). Evenly divide soufflé mixture between ramekins, and place in the preheated oven (middle rack). Turn the oven down to 375°F, and bake soufflés for 30 minutes without opening the oven door. Turn off the oven, leaving the soufflés inside for another 5 minutes. Serve soufflés immediately with the orange compote.

**1** Continue stirring the sticky mixture until it separates from the bottom of the pan into a ball.

**2** Fold in stiffly beaten egg whites very carefully and lightly, preferably with a rubber spatula.

**3** Rotate the ramekins to distribute bread crumbs evenly over the sides and bottoms.

Smooth

# Milk-and-Coffee Zabaglione

MAKES 8 SERVINGS

➤ **For the light zabaglione:**
   **$1/2$ cup milk**
   **2 tbs coffee beans**
   **4 egg yolks**
   **5 tbs sugar**
➤ **For the dark zabaglione:**
   **5 tbs amaretto (optional)**
   **$1/4$ cup hot espresso**
   **4 egg yolks**
   **5 tbs sugar**

🕐 Prep time: 25 minutes
➤ Calories/serving: About 165

1 | For the light zabaglione, heat milk and coffee beans in a saucepan. Before the milk starts to boil, remove from heat and let stand for 2 hours. Then pour through a strainer.

2 | Reheat coffee-milk and keep warm. In a large saucepan, heat water and suspend a smaller bowl over the pan. Place egg yolks and sugar in the bowl, and beat with a wire whisk over low heat until mixture becomes a foamy cream. Gradually stir in warm milk. Remove bowl from the top of the saucepan and set aside.

3 | For the dark zabaglione, combine amaretto and espresso. In a separate bowl, beat egg yolks and sugar over the saucepan, just as you did the light zabaglione, until creamy, gradually adding warm espresso.

4 | Pour dark zabaglione into 8 small dessert bowls. Pour light zabaglione on top and mix slightly.

➤ Variation: Serve zabaglione alone or as a sauce for custards, soufflés, etc.

Melt in Your
Mouth | Smooth

# Mocha Truffles

MAKES ABOUT 35

➤ **$1/4$ cup heavy cream**
   **3 tbs sugar**
   **2 tsp instant coffee**
   **$1 1/2$ cups semisweet chocolate chips**
   **$1/4$ cup coffee liqueur**
   **$1/2$ cup unsalted butter (1 stick)**
   **Cocoa powder for coating**

🕐 Prep time: 1 hour
🕐 Refrigeration time: 5 hours
➤ Calories/serving: About 70

1 | Heat cream over medium heat; add sugar and instant coffee and stir until dissolved. Add chocolate chips and stir over medium heat until melted. Add liqueur, remove from heat, and set aside in a cool place.

2 | As soon as the chocolate mixture has cooled to room temperature, beat softened butter with a hand mixer until fluffy. Stir chocolate mixture into butter one spoonful at a time. Place mixture into the refrigerator for 5 hours or until firm.

3 | Spread cocoa powder in a shallow bowl. Use a spoon to scoop out small balls from the truffle mixture and, using your hands, roll the balls in the cocoa powder. Refrigerate finished truffles to harden (and to store).

### Moist | Easy
# Amaretti Cake

MAKES ONE 9X5-INCH LOAF
PAN (16 SLICES)

➤ 3–4 oz purchased almond
macaroons (or Amarettini
recipe on page 57)

1 3/4 cups flour

4 oz semi-sweet chocolate,
chopped, or 2/3 cup semi-
sweet chocolate chips

2 tsp baking powder

2 tsp cocoa powder

1/2 tsp cinnamon

1 cup butter (2 sticks)

3/4 cup sugar

3 eggs

1/2 cup double-strength
coffee

Grease for the pan

🕐 Prep time: 25 minutes

🕐 Baking time: 50 minutes

➤ Calories per slice: About 250

1 | Preheat the oven to 350°F.
Grease the pan. Place almond
macaroons or Amarettini
cookies in a clean plastic bag,
and crush with a rolling pin.
Combine cookie crumbs,
flour, chocolate, baking
powder, cinnamon, and
cocoa powder.

2 | Using a hand mixer, beat
butter and sugar until fluffy.
Stir in eggs one at a time.

3 | Stir flour mixture and coffee
into batter one spoonful at a
time, alternating between the
two. Pour batter into the pan
and smooth top. Bake in the
oven (middle rack) for 40–50
minutes until golden brown
and a wooden pick inserted
in center comes out clean.

### For Special Occasions
# Mocha Layer Cake

MAKES ONE 9–10-INCH
CAKE (12 PIECES)

➤ 5 eggs, separated

1 cup sugar

6 tbs instant coffee,
divided use

1/4 cup flour

1/4 cup cornstarch

1 tsp baking powder

1 2/3 cup ground almonds

About 1/2 cup coffee
liqueur (may substitute
strong coffee)

4 cups heavy cream

3 1/2 oz coffee-flavored
chocolate, grated

Parchment paper

🕐 Prep time: 50 minutes

🕐 Baking time: 35 minutes

➤ Calories per piece: About 490

1 | Preheat the oven to 350°F.
Gradually add 3/4 cup of the
sugar to the egg whites, beating
until stiff. Dissolve 2 tbs instant
coffee in 2 tbs hot water and
gradually stir into the egg
whites. Blend egg yolks with
a fork and gradually stir into
the beaten egg whites. Combine flour, cornstarch, baking
powder, and almonds. Gently
fold into egg mixture.

2 | Line a 9- or 10-inch
springform pan with parchment paper. Pour in batter
and smooth the top. Bake in
the oven (middle rack) for
30–35 minutes until top feels
springy when lightly touched.
Remove from oven, let cool,
and remove from pan.

3 | Cut cooled cake horizon-
tally into three layers. Brush all
three layers generously with
liqueur. Dissolve remaining
4 tbs instant coffee in 1 tbs
hot water; cool. Whip the
cream, coffee, and remaining
1/4 cup sugar until stiff. Evenly
spread half the cream over
the bottom and middle cake
layers, and stack all three
layers on top of one another.
Spread remaining cream on
top and sides of the cake.
Sprinkle with grated coffee-
flavored chocolate.

# Served with Coffee

A little piece of cake or a sandwich instantly makes any cup of coffee taste that much better. And just as every country has its own coffee specialties, they also have certain treats that go with them. Whether it's hearty Panini or Tramezzini from an Italian coffee bar or a fresh Brioche from a Parisian bistro, you're sure to enjoy it!

| | | | |
|---|---|---|---|
| 43 | Bagels and Lox | 51 | Poppy Seed Crescents |
| 43 | Apple Turnovers | 53 | Brioches |
| 45 | Chicken Tramezzini | 53 | Cappuccino Muffins |
| 45 | Antipasti Vegetable Panini | 54 | Cherry Pie |
| 46 | Club Sandwich | 54 | Spiced Brownies |
| 46 | Goat Cheese Baguette | 57 | Amarettini |
| 49 | Syrup Balls | 57 | Orange Chocolate Cookies |
| 49 | Vanilla Tartlets | | |

# Quick Recipes

## Bagels and Lox

SERVES 4

> 4 bagels | 1 avocado | 1 tbs lemon juice |
> 2 tbs mustard | 2 tbs freshly squeezed
> orange juice | 1 tbs white wine vinegar |
> 2 tbs olive or vegetable oil | 1 tsp freshly
> chopped tarragon | Salt | Pepper |
> 8 oz cream cheese | 7 oz sliced
> smoked salmon

1 | Cut bagels in half horizontally and toast, if desired. Cut avocado in half, remove pit and skin, slice thinly, and drizzle with lemon juice.

2 | Combine mustard, orange juice, vinegar, oil, and tarragon in a shaker jar; shake until well combined. Season to taste with salt and pepper. Spread cheese onto bottom halves of bagels and top with salmon and avocado. Drizzle with vinaigrette and place other bagel halves on top.

## Apple Turnovers

MAKES 6 TURNOVERS

> 1/2 pkg frozen puff pastry dough
> (about 17 oz) | 2 oz marzipan | 3 tbs
> heavy cream | 2 egg yolks | 5 tbs light
> cream cheese | 1 tbs sugar | 1/2 tsp
> cornstarch | 2 apples | Parchment paper

1 | Thaw puff pastry dough. Preheat the oven to 350°F. Crumble marzipan. Combine marzipan, cream, 1 egg yolk, cream cheese, sugar and cornstarch, and beat until smooth. Peel apples, remove cores, dice finely, and stir into cream cheese mixture.

2 | Roll pastry slightly to make into a square. Cut pastry evenly into 6 squares. Spread pastry squares with cheese mixture and fold over diagonally, pressing edges together firmly. Whisk remaining egg yolk and brush onto turnovers. Place on a baking sheet lined with parchment paper and bake in the oven (middle rack) for 20 minutes until golden brown.

43

Can Prepare in Advance

# Chicken Tramezzini

SERVES 4

➤ 2 tbs olive oil
  2 boneless, skinless chicken breasts (approx. ¾ lb)
  Salt and pepper
  1 handful baby spinach
  1 bunch basil
  5 tbs mayonnaise
  1 tbs lemon juice
  Freshly grated nutmeg
  4 large lettuce leaves
  8 slices sandwich bread

🕐 Prep time: 30 minutes
➤ Calories/serving: About 325

1 | In a pan, heat oil and sauté chicken for 8–10 minutes, until brown on all sides. Season with salt and pepper, and let cool.

2 | Rinse spinach and basil, dry, pull off leaves, and finely chop. Combine spinach and basil with mayonnaise and lemon juice. Season to taste with salt, pepper, and nutmeg.

3 | Rinse and dry lettuce. Spread an even layer of the herbed mayonnaise on 4 slices of bread. Slice chicken breast thinly, distribute on bread, and cover with 1 lettuce leaf each. Place remaining bread slices on top, press down lightly, and cut sandwiches diagonally in half.

Vegetarian | Mediterranean

# Antipasti Vegetable Panini

SERVES 4

➤ 2 red bell peppers
  1 eggplant
  5 tbs olive oil
  Salt and pepper
  1 clove garlic
  2 tbs balsamic vinegar
  ½ tsp dried herbes de Provence
  8 oz mozzarella
  4 panini (may substitute baguette rolls)

🕐 Prep time: 25 minutes
🕐 Marinating time: 1 hour
➤ Calories/serving: About 370

1 | Preheat oven broiler. Rinse bell peppers, cut into quarters lengthwise, and clean. Rinse eggplant, clean, and cut crosswise into ⅓-inch thick slices.

2 | Brush a baking sheet with 1 tbs oil. Place eggplant slices on the baking sheet, brush slices with 2 tbs oil, and season with salt and pepper. Place bell peppers on the baking sheet with the cut sides down.

3 | Broil in the oven for 10–15 minutes, turning the eggplant slices once. Remove from oven, let cool, and with a knife strip the peel off the bell peppers.

4 | Peel garlic, squeeze through a press, and combine with remaining oil, balsamic vinegar, and herbs. Marinate eggplant and bell peppers in this mixture for 1 hour.

5 | Slice mozzarella. Cut rolls in half horizontally. Place marinated vegetables and mozzarella on the bottom roll half, season with pepper, and place the other roll half on top.

### American Classic
# Club Sandwich

SERVES 4:

➤ 3 small pickled gherkin

1 tbs capers

1 tbs freshly chopped parsley

6 tbs mayonnaise

Paprika

8 iceberg lettuce leaves

2 tomatoes

12 slices sandwich bread

4 slices cooked ham

4 slices Emmenthaler cheese

🕐 Prep time: 25 minutes

➤ Calories/serving: About 345

1 | Finely chop gherkins and capers. Combine gherkins, capers, parsley, and mayonnaise. Season to taste with paprika.

2 | Rinse and dry lettuce. Rinse tomatoes, dry, remove cores, and slice.

3 | Toast bread and let cool. Spread 8 slices with an even layer of mayonnaise mixture. Top 4 of these slices with ham slices, half the tomatoes, and 4 lettuce leaves. Top the other 4 bread slices with cheese, the remaining tomatoes, and lettuce leaves. Stack slices on top of one another and cover with remaining 4 bread slices. Press together only slightly and cut in half diagonally.

### Vegetarian
# Goat Cheese Baguette

SERVES 4

➤ 7 oz fresh goat cheese

3 oz light cream cheese

1 sprig fresh rosemary, rinsed and chopped

2 tbs honey

2 tbs coarse mustard

1 orange

10 butterhead lettuce leaves

10 cherry tomatoes

Pepper

1 baguette (may substitute 4 baguette rolls)

🕐 Prep time: 20

➤ Calories/serving: About 320

1 | Combine goat cheese, cream cheese, and rosemary. In a separate bowl, stir together honey and mustard.

2 | With a sharp knife, carefully peel orange so that no white membrane remains. Cut into quarters lengthwise and then into small pieces. Rinse and dry lettuce. Rinse tomatoes, cut into quarters, and remove cores.

3 | Cut baguette in half lengthwise. Spread cream mixture on the bottom half and season with pepper. Drizzle with honey-mustard mixture. Distribute lettuce, tomatoes and oranges on top, and cover with top half of baguette. Press down lightly and cut diagonally into 4 equal pieces.

➤ Variation: Instead of goat cheese and rosemary, use cream cheese and tarragon.

*Photo top:* **Club Sandwich**   *Photo bottom:* **Goat Cheese Baguette** ➤

### Middle-Eastern Classic
# Syrup Balls

MAKES ABOUT 25 BALLS

➤ For the dough:
2 1/2 cups flour
1 pinch cinnamon
1 pinch cardamom
1 tsp grated orange zest
1 pkg active dry yeast
(about 1/4 oz)
1 tsp sugar
1/4 cup butter (1/2 stick)
1 egg

➤ For the syrup:
1 cup sugar
1/2 cup honey
1 tbs orange blossom
water (may substitute
lemon juice)
Oil or shortening for
deep frying
Chopped pistachios
for garnish

🕓 Prep time: 1 hour
🕓 Rising time: Over 1 hour
➤ Calories/serving: About 155

1 | For the dough, combine flour, spices, and orange zest, making a well in the center. Stir yeast and sugar into 1/2 cup warm water (about 110°F) and let stand until foamy, about 5 minutes. Pour into the well. Cut softened butter into bits and stir into dough. Cover and let rise for 30 minutes.

2 | Whisk egg, add to dough, and knead on a floured surface until smooth and elastic (add water if dough is too dry). Cover and let rise for another 40 minutes.

3 | For the syrup, combine sugar, honey, and 2/3 cup water in a saucepan. Simmer over medium heat for 5 minutes, stirring often. Stir in orange water; let cool.

4 | Heat frying oil. Shape dough into balls. Fry 4–5 minutes in hot oil until golden, turning once. Drain on paper towels; keep warm. Pour syrup over balls and sprinkle with pistachios.

### Portuguese Classic
# Vanilla Tartlets

MAKES 12 TARTLETS

➤ 2 sheets frozen puff pastry
dough (about 1 lb), or 12
puff pastry tartlet shells
1 cup heavy cream
2 tsp cornstarch
Pulp scraped from
1 vanilla bean
6 egg yolks
1/3 cup sugar
Grated zest of 1 lemon
Flour for the work surface
1 muffin pan with 12 wells

🕓 Prep time: 25 minutes
🕓 Baking time: 10 minutes
➤ Calories/serving: About 270

1 | Thaw pastry dough. Preheat oven to 425°F. Stir cornstarch into 1/4 cup of the cream. In a saucepan, combine remaining cream with vanilla pulp, egg yolks, sugar, and zest; whisk thoroughly.

2 | Stir egg cream over low heat until warm. Stir in cornstarch mixture, and continue heating and stirring until cream thickens (don't boil or the egg yolk will break down). Remove from heat.

3 | Roll out pastry sheets just slightly on a floured surface. From each sheet, cut out circles about 4-inches in diameter, making 12 circles. Rinse a muffin pan with cold water and press pastry into the wells. Pour in mixture and bake (middle rack) for about 10 minutes. Serve slightly warm.

Viennese Classic

# Poppy Seed Crescents

MAKES 10 CRESCENTS

➤ For the dough:

1 pkg active dry yeast (about 1/4 oz)

1/2 cup warm milk (about 110°F)

3 tbs sugar

2 cups flour

1 egg yolk

1/2 cup butter (1 stick)

1 egg for glazing

➤ For the filling:

1/4 cup chopped candied lemon peel

1 can purchased poppy seed filling (about 8 oz)

3 tbs rum (optional)

3 tbs bread crumbs

2 tbs crème fraîche or sour cream

1/2 tsp cinnamon

Parchment paper

🕐 Prep time: 50 minutes

🕐 Standing time: 1 hour

🕐 Baking time: 30 minutes

➤ Calories/serving: About 240

1 | Combine yeast, warm milk, and 1 tbs sugar; let stand until foamy, about 5 minutes. In a large bowl, combine flour and remaining sugar, and form a well in the center. Place egg yolk in the well. Cut softened butter into bits and distribute around the edges.

2 | Add yeast mixture to flour and knead vigorously into a smooth dough. Transfer to a floured bowl, cover, and refrigerate for 30 minutes.

3 | Finely dice candied lemon peel and combine with poppy seed mixture, rum, bread crumbs, crème fraîche, and the cinnamon.

4 | Preheat the oven to 350°F. Knead dough thoroughly on a floured surface and divide into 10 portions. Roll out each portion into an oval with a diameter of about 4 1/2 inches (1). Place a row of filling down the length of each oval. Starting from a longer edge, roll up into crescents (2). Squeeze ends firmly together. Place crescents on a baking sheet lined with parchment paper.

5 | Whisk egg and brush onto crescents. Let dry for 15 minutes, brush on another coating, and let dry for another 15 minutes (3). Bake in the oven (middle rack) for 25–30 minutes until golden brown.

1 Roll out dough into ovals. If necessary, shape them slightly with your hands.

2 From a longer edge, roll up ovals into crescents.

3 Let egg dry well to produce the typical cracks in the surface.

51

French Classic

# Brioches

MAKES 16 BRIOCHES

- ➤ 1 pkg active dry yeast (about ¼ oz)

  3 tbs sugar

  4 cups flour

  ½ cup warm milk (about 110°F)

  ½ tsp salt

  1 tsp grated lemon zest

  4 eggs

  1 cup butter (2 sticks)

  Flour for the work surface

- ➤ For glazing:

  2 egg yolks

  ¼ cup heavy cream

  16 individual brioche molds or deep muffin pans

- ⏱ Prep time: 20 minutes
- ⏱ Rising time: 2 hours and 35 minutes
- ⏱ Baking time: 25 minutes
- ➤ Calories/serving: About 275

1 | Combine yeast, sugar, ¾ cup flour, and ¼ cup warm milk. Cover and let rise for 20 minutes.

2 | In a bowl, combine remaining flour, salt and lemon zest, and form a well in the center. Place eggs in the well. Cut butter into bits and distribute around the edges. Stir in yeast mixture and remaining lukewarm milk. Knead thoroughly for about 8 minutes until smooth and elastic. Transfer to a floured bowl, cover, and let rise in a warm place for 2 hours.

3 | Knead dough thoroughly once more and let rise for another 15 minutes. Preheat oven to 375°F. Grease brioche molds or deep muffin pans.

4 | Divide dough into 16 portions. Take ⅔ of each portion and shape into balls. Place in the molds and make depressions in the centers. Shape remaining ⅓ of dough into smaller balls and press into the depressions. Whisk egg yolks with cream and brush onto the brioches. Bake in the oven (middle rack) for 20–25 minutes until golden brown.

Unusual

# Cappuccino Muffins

MAKES 12 MUFFINS

- ➤ 6 tbs cream cheese

  ¼ cup whole cranberry sauce

  2⅓ cups flour

  2 tbs cocoa powder

  2 tsp baking powder

  1 egg

  ⅔ cup

  ⅞ cup milk

  ⅓ cup vegetable oil

  ¼ cup double-strength cold espresso

  Muffin pan and 12 paper-lined baking cups

- ⏱ Prep time: 15 minutes
- ⏱ Baking time: 25 minutes
- ➤ Calories/serving: About 220

1 | Preheat the oven to 350°F. Line muffin pan with paper baking cups. Combine cream cheese and cranberry sauce; set aside. In a bowl, combine flour, cocoa powder, and baking powder.

2 | Whisk egg and combine with sugar, milk, oil, and espresso. Add to flour mixture and stir.

3 | Pour half the batter into the baking cups. Place about 2 tsp cranberry-cream cheese mixture on top of each, and pour remaining batter on top. Bake in the oven (middle rack) for 20–25 minutes until a wooden pick inserted in center of a muffin comes out clean. Cool in the pan 10 minutes before removing.

American Classic
# Cherry Pie

MAKES ONE 9-INCH PIE OR
SPRINGFORM PAN (8 PIECES)

➤ 2½ cups flour
- ½ cup powdered sugar
- 1 pinch salt
- 12 tbs cold butter (1½ sticks)
- 2 egg yolks
- 2 jars morello cherries (12 oz each, drained weight)
- 7 tbs sugar
- 1 tbs cornstarch
- 1 cup slivered almonds
- 1 tsp vanilla extract
- Grease for the pan
- Flour for the work surface

🕐 Prep time: 30 minutes
🕐 Standing time: 1 hour
🕐 Baking time: 30 minutes
➤ Calories/serving: About 515

1 | Combine flour, powdered sugar, and salt. Add butter cut into bits and blend to form a crumbly mixture. Add egg yolks one at a time. Then add 4–6 tbs ice water and knead into a pliable dough. Set aside in a cool place for 1 hour.

2 | Pour cherries into a strainer and reserve the juice. In a medium saucepan, combine juice, 5 tbs sugar, and cornstarch. Bring to a boil, and boil for 1 minute. Remove from heat and stir in cherries, almonds, and vanilla.

3 | Preheat oven to 375°F. Grease the pan. Roll out about ⅔ of the dough on a floured work surface. Place in the pan and pour cherry filling on top. Roll out remaining dough, place on top of the filling, and pinch edges together firmly. Cut 8 slits in the top in a star pattern and sprinkle with remaining sugar. Bake in the oven (middle rack) for 25–30 minutes or until crust is golden brown and filling is bubbly.

American Classic
# Spiced Brownies

MAKES ONE 8X8-INCH PAN
(16 BROWNIES)

➤ 1 cup pecans
- 1 cup semisweet chocolate chips
- 5 tbs butter
- 1¼ cups flour
- 1½ tsp baking powder
- 1 tsp cinnamon
- 1 tsp grated orange zest
- ¼ tsp allspice
- ¼ tsp nutmeg
- ⅓ cup sugar
- 2 tbs corn syrup
- 2 tbs milk
- 1 tbs vanilla extract
- 1 egg
- Parchment paper

🕐 Prep time: 25 minutes
🕐 Baking time: 30 minutes
➤ Calories/serving: About 180

1 | Preheat the oven to 350°F. Coarsely chop pecans. Melt chocolate and butter in a double boiler, stirring occasionally. Combine flour, baking powder, orange zest, spices, and pecans.

2 | Let chocolate mixture cool slightly. Then one at a time, stir in sugar, corn syrup, milk, and vanilla. Stir in egg. Add flour mixture one spoonful at a time and stir well.

3 | Line pan with parchment paper, pour in batter and smooth top. Bake in the oven (middle rack) for 25–30 minutes. Let cool in the pan. Cut into 2-inch squares.

*Photo top:* Cherry Pie    *Photo bottom:* Spiced Brownies ➤

## Italian Classic
# Amarettini

MAKES ABOUT 25 COOKIES

➤ **7 oz ground blanched almonds (about 1²/₃ cups)**
  **¹/₄ cup sugar**
  **2 egg whites**
  **¹/₂ tsp almond extract**
  **¹/₂ cup powdered sugar**
  **Parchment paper**

🕐 Prep time: 40 minutes
🕐 Drying time: 12 hours
🕐 Baking time: 5 minutes
➤ Calories/serving: About 70

1 | Combine almonds and sugar. Whisk 1 egg white with almond extract and add to almonds. Knead with your hands into a marzipan-like dough.

2 | Using a hand mixer, beat remaining egg white and powdered sugar until smooth and work into almond mixture. Place this mixture in a pastry bag and pipe walnut-sized mounds onto a baking sheet lined with parchment paper. Cover with a kitchen towel and let dry for 12 hours.

3 | Preheat oven to 375°F. Bake in the oven (middle rack) for about 10 minutes or until lightly browned. Cool completely.

## Fruity | Moist
# Orange Chocolate Cookies

MAKES ABOUT 25 COOKIES

➤ **²/₃ cup candied orange peel**
  **²/₃ cup semisweet chocolate chips, or 3¹/₂ oz semi-sweet chocolate**
  **2¹/₂ cups flour**
  **1 tsp baking powder**
  **1 pinch salt**
  **10 tbs butter, softened (1 stick, plus 2 tbs)**
  **³/₄ cup granulated sugar**
  **1 egg**
  **¹/₄ cup freshly squeezed orange juice**
  **Parchment paper**

🕐 Prep time: 25 minutes
🕐 Baking time: 12 minutes
➤ Calories/serving: About 140

1 | Preheat oven to 350°F. Coarsely chop chocolate. Finely dice the candied orange peel.

2 | Combine flour, baking powder and salt, and set aside. In a medium bowl, beat butter and sugar until smooth. Beat in egg.

3 | Stir flour into butter mixture with a spoon. Add orange juice, chopped chocolate, and diced orange. Knead vigorously with your hands into a smooth dough.

4 | Shape dough into about 25 balls, flatten slightly, and place on 2 baking sheets lined with parchment paper. Bake sheets one at a time in the oven for 10–12 minutes (middle rack) until the cookie edges are lightly browned. Remove from the oven and leave on the baking sheet for 10 minutes. Then transfer to a cooling rack to cool.

**TIP** Melt about 7 oz semi-sweet chocolate or 1¹/₄ cups semi-sweet chocolate chips in a double boiler and dip bottoms of the Amarettini into the chocolate. Place dipped Amaretti on a cooling rack chocolate side up to harden.

◄ *In the cup:* **Amarettini**    *On the saucer:* **Orange Chocolate Cookies**

# The ABC's of Coffee

**Biedermeier:** Austrian specialty—a large espresso with apricot liqueur and whipped cream.

**Brauner:** Austrian name for a demitasse of black coffee with a dash of milk or whipped cream. The color varies depending on the amount of milk.

**Café au lait:** French milk-and-coffee drink (recipe on page 7).

**Café noir (or nature):** The small black espresso served in French bistros.

**Caffè:** Usual Italian term for espresso.

**Caffè corretto:** Espresso with a shot of grappa, sambuca, or cognac.

**Caffè latte:** Italian milk-and-coffee drink.

**Cappuccino:** Espresso with milk and topped with foam (recipe on page 7).

**Eispänner:** Austrian specialty—tall glass more than half filled with coffee and topped with whipped cream. In France, this is called a café viennois (Viennese coffee).

Add a shot of rum or cognac and it becomes a Fiaker, named after the horse-drawn coaches in Vienna.

**Espresso:** In Italy, espresso is served small, strong, and black (recipe on page 8). If you want it especially strong, order a ristretto. If you want it even stronger, order a doppio (double). If you prefer it less strong, order a caffè lungo or caffè americano, both consisting of espresso that has been "stretched" with hot water, or a caffè macchiato—espresso "stained" with a spot of milk.

**Kaffee fertig:** In Germany, this is coffee with milk and sugar; in Switzerland, it's coffee with a shot of fruit brandy.

**Kaffee verkehrt:** "Backward coffee"—Viennese name for a mixture that is more milk than coffee.

**Kahve:** Turkish coffee (recipe on page 7).

**Kapuziner:** Austrian espresso with a dash of milk or whipped cream that turns it a shade of brown like the robes of Capuchin monks.

**Maria Theresia:** A cup of Austrian espresso flavored with an orange liqueur.

**Mariloman:** Austrian name for an espresso with a shot of cognac.

**Mazagran:** French specialty—sweetened, iced coffee with maraschino liqueur.

**Melange:** Austrian milk-and-coffee drink (recipe on page 7).

**Obermayer:** A large cup of espresso with a thin layer of cold cream, named after a member of the Vienna Philharmonic.

**Pharisäer:** Northern-German invention—hot coffee and rum topped with whipped cream.

**Schwarzer:** From Austria—plain and simple, a strong little coffee without anything added, also called a Mocca. Add a little hot water and it becomes a Verlängerter; add cold water and it becomes a Konsul.

# Special Coffee Breaks

### German Coffee Bar

➤ This specialty from Bergisches Land in North-Rhine Westphalia, Germany, naturally revolves around good, whole bean coffee, plus fresh waffles with whipped cream and cherries, and if desired, try rice pudding with cinnamon and sugar. For those who want something heartier, black bread with cream cheese or butter, plus honey or apple butter on request—a truly satisfying coffee klatch!

### Italian Coffee Breakfast

➤ A quick espresso snatched in a bar on the way to work is the standard Italian breakfast. It's a little more comfortable when you sit down with your espresso and a panini or tramezzini, and maybe even a little piece of cold pizza topped only with tomato sauce; or, if you're in the mood for something sweet, a small Danish pastry.

### Parisian Morning Coffee

➤ Every morning, the French get going with a bowl of steaming café au lait. It is also common to dip a croissant into your coffee bite by bite. If you want a little more than that, you can have your coffee with a fresh brioche or baguette, plain or with marmalade. A little later in the day, there's nothing like coffee with an éclair or petit four.

### Viennese Coffee House

➤ Freshly brewed coffee with whipped cream, plus dessert, make up the Viennese coffee break. Desserts can include a doughnut, cream puffs, Strudel, various Danish pastries, and poppy seed, nut or vanilla crescents, and the famous Sachertorte or Linzertorte.
To produce that authentic Viennese coffee house atmosphere, just add mellow strains of a violin.

### New York Breakfast

➤ In addition to the usual filter coffee, which usually comes with endless and free refills, coffees flavored with syrups are all the rage. And if you don't want to carry it to work in a paper cup, you can have your coffee with breakfast: Eggs and bacon, pancakes or waffles with syrup, bagels with hearty toppings, or sweet doughnuts and muffins.

### Middle Eastern Coffee Dessert

➤ Strong, black, and as highly sweetened as possible, a small mocha is the perfect close to a Middle-Eastern feast. And the delicacies and baked goods served with it are every bit as sweet, including syrup-soaked baklava or fritters (see Syrup Ball recipe on page 49), pastries made with lots of nuts, figs and honey, or perhaps a piece of halva.

## A

**Advocaat**
ice cream coffee 24
mocha brandy cocktail 27
**Almonds**
amarettini 57
cherry pie 54
coffee 13
syrup (basic recipe) 9
Amaretti cake 41
Amarettini 57
**Amaretto**
almond coffee 13
milk-and-coffee zabaglione 39
tiramisu 33
Antipasti vegetable panini 45
Apple turnovers 43

## B

Bagels and lox 43
Banana coffee shake 23
**Brandy**
and chocolate coffee 19
mocha flip 27
mocha cocktail 27
Brioche 53
Brownies, spiced 54

## C

Café au lait (preparation) 7
Café brulôt 19
**Cake**
amaretti 41
mocha layer 41
**Cappuccino**
muffins 53
preparation 7
Caramel syrup (basic recipe) 9
**Cheese**
antipasti vegetable panini 45
club sandwich 46
goat, baguette 46
**Cherries**
Black Forest, coffee 15
pie 54
syrup (basic recipe) 9
Chicken tramezzini 45
**Chocolate**
amaretti cake 41

espresso cream with
raspberries 29
mocha layer cake 41
mocha truffles 39
mousse au café 34
orange cookies 57
spiced brownies 54
Viennese, coffee 15
white, latte 21
**Coconut**
coffee toffees 29
cool cocoa-, coffee 23
**Coffee**
cultivation 4
flan 34
filter 65
garnishing 65
German 59
Italian 59
Middle Eastern 59
New York 59
origin 4
Parisian 59
plants 5
preparation 5
processing 5
serving 65
storing 65
syrup (basic recipe) 9
Viennese 59
**Coffee, cold**
Advocaat ice cream 24
banana shake 23
cool coca-coconut 23
herbal cocktail 27
ice cream 11
marzipan 24
**Coffee, hot**
After Eight mint 15
almond 13
Black Forest cherry 15
brandy and chocolate 19
café brulôt 19
Irish19
Kaiser melange 21
mocha soufflé with orange
compote 37

Spanish 16
Swiss plum 11
Viennese chocolate 15
**Coffee, instant**
coconut coffee toffees 29
mocha layer cake 41
mocha truffles 39
mousse au café 34
**Coffee liqueur**
Advocaat ice cream 24
cool cocoa-coconut 23
espresso cream with
raspberries 29
Mexican 16
mocha layer cake 41
mocha soufflé with orange
compote 37
mocha truffles 39
mousse au café 34
spiced granita 31
**Cognac**
café brulôt 19
caffè cotta 33
coffee flan 34
kaiser melange 21
Cookies, orange chocolate 57
Cream and milk 64

## E

**Eggs**
amaretti cake 41
apple turnovers 43
brioches 53
coffee flan 34
coffee nog 21
kaiser melange 21
milk-and-coffee zabaglione 39
mocha flip 27
mocha layer cake 41
mocha parfait 31
mocha soufflé with orange
compote 37
mousse au café 34
poppy seed crescents 51
spiced brownies 54
syrup balls 49
tiramisu 33
vanilla tartlets 49

Espresso
cream with raspberries 29
French presses 6
machines 6
preparation 8, 65
stove top makers 6, 8
Espresso, cold
cappuccino muffins 53
cream with raspberries 29
mandarin-orange mocha
smoothie 23
mocha flip 27
mocha latte on the rocks 24
spiced coffee granita 31
tiramisu 33
Espresso, hot
caffè cotta 33
coffee nog 21
ginger coffee 16
hot coffee shot 27
latte macchiato 13
milk-and-coffee zabaglione 39
white chocolate latte 21

Flan, coffee 34
Flavorings
caramel syrup 9
coffee syrup 9
fruit syrup 9
Frother, milk 6
Fruit syrup (basic recipe) 9

Ginger coffee 16
Herbal liqueur
coffee cocktail 27
hot coffee shot 27

Ice cream
Advocaat coffee 24
banana coffee shake 23
coffee 11
marzipan coffee 24
Irish coffee 19

Latte macchiato 13
Liqueurs and syrups 65
Lox, bagels and 43

Mandarin-orange mocha
smoothie 23
Maple syrup
banana coffee shake 23
white chocolate latte 21
Marzipan
apple turnovers 43
coffee 24
Mascarpone
espresso cream with
raspberries 29
tiramisu 33
Melange
Kaiser 21
preparation 7
Mexican coffee 16
Milk and cream 64
Mocha
brandy cocktail 27
flip 27
latte on the rocks 24
layer cake 41
mandarin-orange, smoothie 23
parfait 31
soufflé with orange compote 37
truffles 39
Mousse au café 34
Muffins, cappuccino 53

Oranges
chocolate cookies 57
mocha soufflé with, compote 37
Orange liqueur
café brulôt 19
mandarin-, mocha smoothie 23
mocha soufflé with, compote 37

Pie, cherry 54
Raspberries, espresso cream
with 29

Sandwich(es)
antipasti vegetable panini 45
bagels and lox 43
chicken tramezzini 45
club 46
goat cheese baguette 46

Soufflé, mocha with orange
compote 37
Spanish coffee 16
Spices 64
Syrup(s)
and liqueurs 65
balls 49
caramel syrup 9
coffee syrup 9
fruit syrup 9

Tartlets, vanilla 49
Tiramisu 33
Toffees, coconut coffee 29
Truffles, mocha 39
Turkish coffee (preparation) 7, 64

Vanilla
syrup (basic recipe) 9
tartlets 49
Vegetable, panini anipasti 45
Viennese
chocolate coffee 15
coffee house 59
mélange (preparation) 7
Whiskey
coffee nog 21
herbal coffee cocktail 27
Irish coffee 19

Yeast dough
brioches 53
poppy seed crescents 51
syrup balls 49
Yogurt
banana coffee shake 23
mandarin-orange mocha
smoothie 23

**ABBREVIATIONS**

lb = pound
oz = ounce
tsp = teaspoon
tbs = tablespoon

## The Author

**Tanja Dusy** lives in Munich. Her passion for cooking led this TV editor of a cooking show to become a freelance journalist and a cook in a catering business, finally allowing her to turn her hobby into a career.

## The Photographer

**Jörn Rynio** works as a photographer in Germany. His customers include national and international magazines, book publishers, and ad agencies. All the recipe photos in this book were produced in his studio with the energetic support of his food stylist, Petra Speckmann.

## Photo Credits

Stockfood, Munich: pages 4 and 5

All others: Jörn Rynio, Germany

Published originally under the title Kaffee und Espresso: die Kaffeebar zu Hause © 2003 Gräfe und Unzer Verlag GmbH, Munich.
English translation for the U.S. market © 2004, Silverback Books, Inc.

Program director: Doris Birk
Editor: Lisa M. Tooker, Rosemary Mark, Alessandra Redies,
Translator: Christie Tam
Readers: Tanja Germann and Mischa Gallé
Typesetting: Appl, Wemding
Layout, typography and cover design: Independent Medien Design, Munich
Production: Patty Holden, Maike Harmeier

Printed in China

ISBN 1-930603-39-8

# Enjoy Other Quick & Easy Books

1 Pan— 50 Muffins

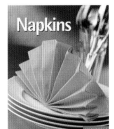
Napkins

Christmas Cookies

Fast Italian

Margit Proebst

Sauces and Dips

Irresistible Fondue

Angelika Illies

Cooking for Two

Cornelia Adam

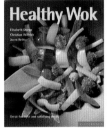
Healthy Wok

Elisabeth Doepp
Christian Willrich
Doris Reiner

Great for light and satisfying meals

Antje Gruener
Grilling

Andreas Fürtmayr
Sushi

Classic ideas from Japan
and new fusion sushi
Home-made perfectly

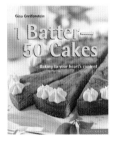
Gina Greifenstein
1 Batter— 50 Cakes

Baking to your heart's content

Cooking in Clay

Healthy Recipes with Great Flavor

Erika Casparek-Türkkan

1 Noodle, 50 Sauces

Everyday Pasta • Old and New Italian Dishes
Noodle biography • 10 Tips for Success

Doris Muliar
Cocktails for Drivers

100% Enjoyment

Antipasti and Tapas

Mediterranean Appetizers
Cornelia Schinharl

Soups

Classic to Contemporary

Sebastian Dickhaut

Claudia Schmidt
Raclette

New Recipes with Cheese Primer and Party Dips

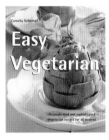
Cornelia Schinharl
Easy Vegetarian

Deconomized and sophisticated –
Vegetarian recipes for all seasons

Cornelia Adam
Garlic

Sophisticated Recipes with the Favorite
Spice of the Mediterranean Regions
Spicy, Tangy, Fine Delicacies International

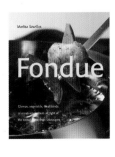
Marlisa Szwillus
Fondue

Cheese, vegetable, meat kinds
of meat—you'll have all right at
the table. Even than Silvester.

Sebastian Dickhaut
Casseroles

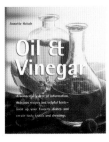
Annette Heisch
Oil & Vinegar

A wonderful source of information,
delicious recipes and helpful hints—
liven up your favorite dishes and
create tasty sauces and dressings.

Cornelia Adam
Quiche

Delicious, savory pies with
vegetables, meat, poultry or
fish—serve for all occasions.

### THE WATER

- If you can, brew your coffee with filtered water containing as little lime as possible or even uncarbonated mineral water.
- Pour the water over the coffee when the water is hot, but no longer boiling (the ideal temperature is about 200°F). If the water is too hot, it increases the coffee's acidity; if it's too cold, it makes the coffee taste bitter.

# Guaranteed Perfect Coffee and Espresso

### TURKISH COFFEE

- Use only light roast coffee ground as finely as possible.
- Use about 2 tsp ground coffee and $1/2$ cup water per serving.
- Constantly stir the coffee with a teaspoon while heating so it will develop a nice foam.

### SPICES

- Simply brew ground spices such as cinnamon, cloves, cardamom, or a pinch of nutmeg along with the ground coffee.
- Whole spices such as cloves and cinnamon sticks, or even fresh ginger or orange zest, are great for cold drinks. Pour hot coffee over the top and let them steep a while.

### MILK AND CREAM

- Try to use low-fat milk because whole milk hides the coffee aroma.
- Heat milk in a saucepan and add it hot to the coffee.
- It's better to use whipped cream that's not too stiffly beaten because cream that is less stiff blends more easily with the coffee.